THE
ENOCH GENERATION

THE SECRETS OF WALKING WITH GOD

BY HUMPHREY MTANDWA

NH

NEW HERITAGE
PRESS

The Enoch Generation 1ˢᵗ Edition

Published by New Heritage Press, Harare

Copyright © by Humphrey Mtandwa 2015

The author asserts his moral right to be identified as the author of this work.

ISBN 978-0-79746572-5

Edited by Phillip Kundeni Chidavaenzi

Cover design by Francis Chidavaenzi

Set in Calisto MT by New Heritage Press

Layout by New Heritage Press. Harare

Pastor Humphrey Mtandwa is an anointed minister of the gospel, sent to this generation with a mandate to make the voice of God clear to all. He preaches and teaches the Word of God with simplicity and power. Together with his wife, Pastor Grace Mtandwa, he desires to see a generation that will walk in a perfect relationship with God.

CONTENTS

FOREWORD

Having known Pastor Humphrey Mtandwa for nearly 10 years, I have been a first-hand witness of his love for the Lord and his passion for God's Word.

In the early years, around 2006, on several occasions I was honoured to sit under his teaching and I have always been amazed by his deep insight into the scriptures, and the revelations that God had always deposited into his spirit. It therefore came to me as a high honour when Pastor Mtandwa asked me to edit and publish this this book.

Here is a man I have known for many years, and I can testify to how he, just like the Enoch he alludes to in this book, walks with God.

This is a handy book in which he shares the secrets of how to walk with the Lord, that in itself a desire of many believers. Unfortunately many have not known how to engage in this walk. I have no doubt that whoever reads this book will be blessed, and their life will never be the same again.

Pastor Phillip Kundeni Chidavaenzi
Divine Insight Teaching Ministry

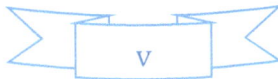

Acknowledgments

I want to acknowledge Apostle George and Prophetess Edwina Nyashanu of Worship Yeshua Ministries, under whom I serve, for believing and investing in the call of God upon my life.

I also want to salute my wife, Grace, who is such a blessing in my life.

CHAPTER 1

A CALL TO FELLOWSHIP

WHEN God created man, he created him for fellowship. Throughout the Bible, we see God's pursuit of man and man's response to God's call. The Bible begins by relating how God created the world and man's fall from grace.

The book of Genesis speaks of the generations of man, from Cain to Seth. In Genesis 4:26, man begins to call again on the Lord. Within that period, man did not fellowship with God as He desired. When man was created, it was so that he would commune and fellowship with God. The true purpose of man was to fellowship with his Creator. God was looking for a man who could seek His presence and desire fellowship as he did. God was robbed of the desired relationship He wanted with man because of man's fall.

This story becomes an amazing love story, with God after man's soul and man disappointing God. This is portrayed in the book of Hosea who is instructed by God to go marry a wife of whoredom. When Gomer later becomes unfaithful, God again instructs Hosea to take her. This story is a perfect picture of God's love for His children and how He continually pursues them even when they fall into sin.

> *"...then said the Lord unto me, go yet, love a woman beloved of her friend, yet an adulteress according to the love of the Lord toward the children of Israel who look to other gods and love flagons of wine."*
>
> **Hosea 3:1**

The children of Israel continuously walked in sin, refusing to hearken to the voice of God, yet He would go after them again and again.

> *"Ye have not chosen me, but I have chosen you and ordained you that you should bring forth fruit and that your fruit should remain: whatsoever ye*

shall ask of the father in my name he shall give it you."

John 15:16

Having a relationship with God is not something that man decided on. It was God who chose man. What is interesting is that there was a single man long after Adam, with sin having spread its tentacles across the world, who chose not to follow the steps of his fathers but looked for this God who had created them.

The Bible gives scant detail about this man called Enoch, but stresses that he walked with God and as he walked with God, he was translated that he did not see death.

Enoch's generation, the seventh from Adam, was later destroyed by the flood.

According to the biblical record, Enoch was the first man after the fall to fellowship with God. What is quite interesting is that the Bible does not divulge much information about this man's relationship with God. But is quite clear that this relationship was significant and as believers we can draw many priceless lessons from it.

DESIRE TO WALK WITH GOD

The same way you desire to walk with God is the same way He desires to walk with you. God is calling each of us to the same kind of fellowship he had with Enoch.

For us, the walk can be even greater in that when Enoch walked with God, the sin nature was still a part of man and he did not have the Holy Spirit in His fullness.

But in our case, the sin nature has been dealt with at the cross. We have the Bible as a manual to live by and the Holy Spirit to lead us in all things.

An important aspect that I want you to understand is that because we are the New Testament church filled with the Holy Spirit in His fullness, we can achieve a greater fellowship with God than the one Enoch had. Imagine having an intimate relationship with the Creator of the world and the benefits of such a relationship! It's huge!

THE CALL TO FELLOWSHIP

"By faith Enoch was translated that he should not see death and was not found because God had translated him: for before his translation he had this testimony that he had pleased God."

Hebrews 11:5

The scripture says by faith Enoch was taken up into heaven bodily. He did not use the entryway of death like every other human being besides Moses and Jesus.

Although Enoch had an intimate relationship with God, we have a greater call through Jesus Christ's sacrifice at the cross and God is calling all believers to fellowship with Him. The voice of God can be so clear if you desire it to be in your life.

What type of relationship did God have with Enoch? Did they spend the day talking and if the answer is yes, what did they talk about? Did God take him to heaven and show him all that He had created? Whatever it was, you can have a greater relationship

---

UNDERSTANDING FELLOWSHIP

What does it mean to fellowship or to walk with God as Enoch did? Does it mean you just walk into heaven?

> *"I knew a man in Christ above four-teen years ago (whether in the body, I cannot tell; or out of the body, I cannot tell: God knoweth;) such as one caught up to the heaven."*
> **2 Corinthians 12:2**

Paul here speaks of a man who walked in-to heaven. If you study closely the life of Paul, you begin to understand what is required of you to have fellowship with God that results in you being translated into heaven. Paul speaks of how he was taken up into the third heaven but uses the third-person narrative as if speaking of someone else. (Elijah is another man who walked with the Lord).

But unlike Enoch and Elijah, the man of whom Paul speaks came back to earth. They are other men that history has not told us of and you can be one of them. Are you ready to be translated (raptured). Paul later on in his epistles says it is gain to die, meaning when you visit heaven, you may never want to come back. I believe that is what happened to Enoch.

QUALIFIED FOR FELLOWSHIP

Every believer is called to fellowship with God. As I have highlighted earlier, when God created man, it was primarily so that He could fellowship with him. We read in Genesis 3:8 that God came down to fellowship with man:

"...and they heard the voice of the Lord God walking in the garden in the cool of the day. And Adam and his wife hid themselves from the presence of the Lord God amongst the trees of the garden."

God was seeking out Adam and Eve so that He could fellowship with them. Enoch, being the seventh from Adam, showed us the results of fellowship with God: courtesy of his fellowship with God, he was translated and did not taste death. God is calling you to this fellowship and you should tell yourself that you qualify for this divine fellowship. The same way in which God came walking in the garden is the same way he is walking in our world today. He wants to fellowship with every person on this earth and has shown us through the Bible how this can be achieved. The question is: what's separating you from this fellowship? It is either the sin nature of the unregenerate man, or the believer's sinful habits.

SIN BREAKS FELLOWSHIP

Romans 5:17, speaks on the call to fellowship. Let's start by looking at it together.

"...for by one man's offence death reigned by one; much more they which receive abundance of grace and of the gift of righteousness shall rein in life by one, Jesus Christ.)"

Romans 5:17

Sin separated man from his privilege of fellowship. Because of Adam's sin, man was separated from God but God, through Jesus Christ, has reconciled man unto Himself. Because of the cross, we now have access to the Father. As believers, we have been called to fellowship and it's your responsibility to seek after God's heart and desire intimacy with Him.

The first step is accepting Jesus Christ as Lord over your life. You cannot experience the fullness of God if you do not know His Son as your Lord and Saviour. The cross has given you access into His presence. There is no other way to God but only through Jesus.

Having grown up in a Christian home, I thought I was a Christian. Although I was baptised according to the traditions of man and church, I lacked revelation about why I was doing it. More than ten years passed and I still thought I was a Christian. Then I was introduced to Jesus in a cell group meeting. I confessed His Lordship over my life and accepted Him as my Lord. That I went to church or I was born in a family of church goers does not guarantee salvation. It's about a confession of faith in the cross and that Jesus came and died for you.

The story of Apollos shows us that a man can even be a teacher of the word but lack full knowledge that leads to salvation.

"And a certain Jew named Apollos, born at Alexandra, an eloquent man and mighty in the scriptures, came to Ephesus. [25] This man was instructed in the way of the Lord; and being fervent in the spirit, he spake and taught diligently the things of the Lord, knowing only the baptism of John [26] and he began to speak boldly in the synagogue: whom Aquila and Priscilla had heard, they took him unto them and expounded unto him the way of God more perfectly."

Acts 18: 24-27

This is very profound and demonstrates the importance of preaching salvation to all men.

HOW DO I GET SAVED?

"… that if thou shalt confess with thy mouth the Lord Jesus and shalt believe in thine heart that God hath raised him from the dead, thou shalt be saved."

Romans 10:9

The first call is a call to salvation. This is a call to every person on this earth. The scripture above demonstrates how salvation is received – through believing with the heart and then confessing with the mouth. There is no other way given to men by which they can receive salvation.

If you have not received Jesus Christ as your Lord and Saviour, you have to do that now, and I am giving you that opportunity. So, I want you to say out the prayer of salvation on the next page.

Don't just say it off your head. Let it be meaningful, from right deep down in your heart. That is how it can have an impact on your life.

SALVATION PRAYER

"Father I come to you in the name of Jesus. Today, I accept that Jesus came and He died for me. Today, I declare that He was resurrected for my justification and I am a now born again. I am now a child of God. Amen!"

IS BELIEF IN JESUS ENOUGH?

The moment you confess the Lordship of Jesus over your life, the sin nature is dealt with and a new life begins. This is a spiritual life. It's the walk of the spirit.

The implication of this new life is that you no longer reason out things the same way you did before. Your reasoning (in the soul) must now submit to your spirit where the Spirit of the Lord now indwells you.

Experienced believers might say this is basic and try to skip it but please, pay attention!

GOD CHOSE ENOCH...

The Bible makes only three references to Enoch yet his life was beyond the three instances mentioned. When you look at his son and the meaning of his name, Methuselah, you realise that his life was more than want we read in scripture. The name Enoch means teaching or commencement. Methuselah means after death, judgment follows. When you look at the life of Enoch, his son's name meant when he dies the judgment of God shall begin. The name spoke of the flood of Noah.

Enoch also spoke of Jesus' return thousands of years before he even came on the earth. He had insight and understood a lot of things. Imagine if all believers could walk like Enoch. When you fellowship with God, you begin to think and act like Him. The generation of believers that fellowships with God will start thinking and acting like God. This is the generation that shall see the rapture. Heaven or rapture is not a rescue mission but Christ is coming for a triumphant church, a glorious church.

The old-time preachers spoke as if heaven was for a defeated church but heaven is for those who would have lived above sin and all the temptations of this world, being perfected by the cross of Christ.

HINDRANCES TO THE WALK

"They that observe lying vanities for-sake their own mercy."

Jonah 2:8

I remember a vision I once had. I was in a dark room and angels appeared in the room. As I looked, I knew they were of God. I looked again at a distant object and saw the devil. I began to focus on him and as I did, he became bigger and bigger than the angels. The angels vanished instantly and I could no longer see them. Fear crept into me and one of the angels reappeared and said to me, "Do not observe lying vanities."

The devil immediately vanished into thin air. If Jonah had focused on his situation while he was in the belly of the fish, he would not have walked out. He had to stop looking at his situation and begin to worship. As he worshipped, he was delivered.

The walk of the spirit requires trust in God and His word even in the face of opposition. The Bible warns against observing lying vanities.

When you observe lying vanities, you will be looking at the shadows or the tricks of the enemy until you no longer see the grace of God.

The Enoch generation will have resistance because they do not observe vanities. They look at the word and put the word first. They use kingdom principles to achieve success. They do not walk according to the set the world systems but practice godly principles in daily life situations.

It's a choice to walk with God and this is a call to walk with God. When one walks with God, they live a holy and godly life.

They live according to what the word says and don't allow the world to influence their walk of faith.

THE ENOCH GENERATION

Jesus is not coming for a defeated church. Heaven is not a rescue plan. When Jesus returns or rapture occurs, we should have demonstrated to the world what it means to walk with God.

When one walks with God, he walks with power and authority and subjects his environment to yield to what he wants. He does not live according to what his environment wants.

This is a call to every believer and it is a call to the bride of Christ because Christ is coming for his bride.

The Bible says the bride has made herself ready and is without blemish. This is a call to all believers to fellowship with the Spirit of God. He desires to fellowship with us because it is part of His ministry in our lives.

BENEFITS OF FELLOWSHIP

"...children in whom was no blemish, but well favoured and skillful in all wisdom, and cunning in knowledge, and understanding, and such had ability in them to stand in the king's palace, and whom they might teach the learning of the Chaldean's."

Daniel 1: 4

When you look at the life and ministry of Daniel, you realise that God will stand with you and grant you favour if you stand on his word. Daniel was the administrative assistant (in our day this means Prime Minister) in the land of Babylon, which was the strongest nation at that time.

He served four different kings. God gave him wisdom so that he could interpret dreams and visions. The most amazing part about his story is that he is the perfect picture of the Enoch generation, man of wisdom and skill.

In Genesis chapters 5 to 10, we see that Noah was another perfect example when you look at the level of ingenuity the level and craftiness in which he walked. In that generation, the world was corrupt but Noah walked with God as his great-great-grandfather Enoch did.

I believe he could have learnt about Enoch from his fathers. Just like Noah, you can be innovative and be ahead of your generation if you trust in God and tap into his vast reserve of knowledge. Jesus is coming for those who are a part of the world but not influenced by the world. These are people influencing the world for the Kingdom.

We are called to be separate from the world, meaning we are not influenced by the world or it systems. If the company you work for is not a Christian company, do they promote Christian values or you are forced to compromise like Lot did in Sodom. If your country is led by non-believers, are they passing laws or regulations that support or promote Christian values?

We should be in the leading roles in all positions of influence in the world so we can promote true Christian values. Soon after the invention of the television, the early church would call it Satan's box instead of finding ways to take a hold of it and control it.

As Christians, we are part of the world and we should study the trends in technological advancement so that we lead and fully control all these areas. We are in the age of the internet, but where is the church? It's time we take over. Jesus is coming back soon.

Have you accepted the call to fellowship, the call to a higher walk with God? Just put your name on the scripture below and meditate on it.

> *"By faith [Humphrey] was translated that he should not see death and was not found because God had translated him: for before his translation he had this testimony that he had pleased God."*
>
> **Hebrews 11:5**

CHAPTER 2

THE BRIDE OF CHRIST

T HE church is not yet the wife of Christ but the bride of Christ. Revelations 19:7 says, *"For the marriage of the Lamb is come, and his wife hath made herself ready…"* Jesus Christ is coming for a church that has made itself ready, a church that is perfect. The moment the church begins to walk in perfection, that is the season for rapture.

Enoch was translated because he had a perfect relationship with God and as he walked in this perfection, he was translated so that he did not see death.

Ephesians 4:13 also spells out the call to the believer.

"Till we all come to the unity of faith and of the knowledge of the son of

God, unto a perfect man, unto the stature of the fullness of Christ."

Ephesians 4:13

UNITY OF THE FAITH

The Word of God is the voice of God and if you are to understand God, you need to understand his Word. When Jesus called us to be his bride, he left us his book of law that we may understand what our husband requires from us. The Bible is the manual that God has given us that we may prepare to be the wife of Christ. Mathew 25: 1-13 tells the story of 10 virgins. The five wise virgins were prepared for the groom. This is the same call for all believers to understand and get ready for the coming of the Lord.

God is calling us to make his word Lord over our lives. I believe men and women will be raised that will show the body of Christ what it means to walk perfectly as Christians. And you are one of these men and women.

These individuals as they walk they will begin to draw disciples to Christ they will walk in perfection like Enoch. The Enoch generation is that of men and women that will walk in perfection.

We also see this call to every believer in Jude 14-15. This was also prophesied before, that the Lord was coming with ten thousand of his saints to execute judgment upon all that are ungodly and the deeds which they have committed.

Believers who walk in perfection have been called to demonstrate the character of God. When you spend time with a person you begin to think and act like him. When you spend time with God, you begin to think and act like him. Jesus said He did what He saw His Father doing.

These men and women are individuals whom God will put in positions of influence. As they execute their responsibilities, they will do it with God-like character. They will walk in the power of God's Spirit. They will manifest this power of God in their environment. This is the same power that made Enoch walk perfectly with God and this pleased the Father so much that He took him up to heaven bodily. You must walk like Enoch. You must walk like Jesus.

> *"And in the days of these kings shall the God of heaven set up a kingdom which shall never be destroyed and the kingdom shall not be left to other people but it shall break and consume all these kingdoms and it shall stand forever for as much as thou sawest that the stone was cut out of the mountain without hands, and that in break in pieces the iron, the clay, the silver and the gold the great God hath made known to the king what shall come to pass here after: and the dream is certain and the interpretation thereof sure."*
>
> **Daniel 2: 44-45**

> *"...therefore he shall divide the spoil with the mighty."*
>
> **Isaiah 53:12**

In his interpretation of Nebuchadnezzar's dream, Daniel speaks of the rock that was cut without hands and how the rock filled the whole world and as it grew, Jesus came and he was that rock that was cut without hands. But the rock's influence still has to grow. The Prophet Isaiah also speaks of how the saints shall prolong the days of Jesus. The church is the body of Christ and the arm of the Lord to execute judgment upon the world.

Daniel said when the rock smashed the statue, it was reduced to chaff. That is the character of the bride of Christ or the Enoch generation. When they begin to walk in power, they will cause the world systems to be turned to chaff. The political world needs men and women who know and fear God and can govern nations using God's principles.

These will include businessmen and women who will uphold godly standards in the marketplace and in the church, ministers who will be able to teach and groom leaders that will take over the world and demonstrate the character of God.

These individuals will begin to control all the major positions in the world demonstrating the power of the Spirit. As they do this they will please God and he will translate them. As they fellowship, they will demonstrate the true nature and quality of the God we serve. The world has looked at Christianity as a poor man's religion for far too long. Are you ready to demonstrate to the world that a walk of the spirit is a walk of power?

The Enoch generation is made up of individuals that are going to execute judgment meaning they will demonstrate what God has expected of man from the beginning. God has called man to fellowship. It's not possible to fellowship with God and his presence does not rub off onto you. You cannot remain the same.

When you walk with God, you qualify for translation. God is looking for a man and woman who can separate themselves from the world and begin to pray and study his Word and fast. These are believers ready to walk in fellowship with him, men and women who will seek God's face for every situation of life and choose to live for God's kingdom and purpose.

Mathew 5:3 says blessed are the poor in spirit for theirs is the kingdom of God. These people are not poor in that they lack material wealth, but they have realised what they are and what they have belong to God. A certain man of God said if such a man has an expensive watch and God instructs him to give it away, he does as instructed without thinking twice. Even if the person is a millionaire, he realises that all he has belongs to God.

The Enoch generation is rich, but understands that wealth belongs to God. I have seen many businessmen whom God had elevated forgetting that God was responsible for their success and wealth.

In the book of Daniel, we learn that kings are elevated into office by God and do not come by their own strength, meaning positions and wealth are ordained by God. The Enoch generation is a group of believers who are able to stand and acknowledge God publicly in their world of influence.

I want to see world presidents who can stand and proclaim Christ. These will not compromise by voting in legislation that promotes ungodly values and practices such as the rage of the moment, homosexuality, which has since been legalised in some countries across the world.

The Bible, in several scriptures, speaks strictly against homosexuality.

CAN THE BRIDE BE PERFECT?

> *"Go ye therefore and teach all nations, baptizing them in the name of the Father, and of the Son and of the Holy Ghost, teaching them to observe all things whatsoever I have commanded you and lo, I am with you alway, even unto the end of the world. Amen."*
>
> ### *Mathew 28:19-20*

The mandate has been given to make disciples. Those that Enoch said will come with the Lord to execute judgment are people that will have walked in authority on this earth. In 1 Corinthians 6, Paul asked,

> *"Do you not know you shall judge angels?"*
>
> ### *1 Corinthians 6:3*

Then he said how can you judge angels if you cannot judge things pertaining to this world.

So as these individuals execute judgment, they will lead many and as many follow, the body will be ready to walk perfectly before the Lord. The bride will follow these leaders until the world cannot contain the bride of Christ.

Rapture will not occur because the Lord would have had mercy on the world, but it will be triggered by effects caused by this last church. They will have so much life that this cursed world will not be able to contain it. The fish had to vomit Jonah because he refused to observe lying vanities. He worshiped God in the belly of that fish. Hell could not contain Jesus because of the power and authority he had. In the same vein, the world will not be able to contain the last church.

Rapture is not a rescue plan but a translation of the victorious church, the triumphant church of Christ.

The word of God must have Lordship over your spirit. Because of the nature of our minds, we have disallowed God's word to renew our thinking. We have to allow the word of God to direct us. The first step is salvation.

The second step is allowing the word of God to govern the way you think. Whenever God wanted to change any person, he would send his word.

In this generation, we have the Bible as our guide and the more we meditate on the word the more we become what the word of God says. Look closely at this scripture and apply what you learn from it.

> *"This book of the law shall not depart out of thy mouth; but thou shalt meditate therein day and night, that thou mayest observe to do according to all that is written therein: for then thou shalt make thy way prosperous and then thou shalt have good success."*
> **Joshua 1:8**

The scripture teaches us that the word has to be in your mind day and night and on your lips. The secret is fellowship with the word until you begin to speak and talk scripture.

> *"By faith Enoch was translated that he should not see death and was not found because God had translated*

him: for before his translation he had this testimony that he had pleased God."

Hebrews 11: 5

Allow that scripture to be a song in your heart. I now know the secret to walking like Enoch. It's having the word in my heart and telling the world who God has said I am.

This is a call to every believer to turn the world systems to chaff and demonstrate God in your sphere of influence in your area of calling.

CHAPTER 3

THE BRIDE AND THE SPIRIT

T HE bride cannot be raptured without the Spirit. There is a call to unity between the Spirit of God and the bride of Christ that we must heed as believers.

> *"And the Spirit and the bride say, Come. And let him that heareth say, Come. And let him that is athirst come. And whosoever will, let him take the water of life freely."*
> **Revelations 22: 17**

The bride and the Spirit must walk in unity of faith. The church has to be yielded to the desires of God's Spirit.

"For we know that the whole creation groaneth in pain together until now."
Romans 8:22

The Enoch generation will release creation by manifesting the character of God. The Enoch generation will be a manifestation of God's virtues and excellences. They are to bring deliverance to creation.

Because of the blessing that was upon Enoch as he walked the earth, he sired a son that stopped the judgment of God in his generation up until his death. The rod of Aaron budded because of the presence of God. Let his presence manifest in you to the extent that homes, businesses, churches and nations are transformed. If the bride fellowships with the Spirit God will manifest himself.

The Enoch generation has a relationship with God through his Spirit. The early church walked in power but the power that I am talking about here exceeds that of the early church. Technology has evolved from the first inventions. When an airplane was invented, it could only travel a limited distance and could only carry a limited number of people. But because the manufacturer of our time took time to study the first model, he was able to develop it further beyond the understanding of the inventors. The same applies to our walk of faith the apostles wrote down all they did so we can learn from them and as we learn from where there left the present day church can walk in greater power because we can learn from the early church what they did right. Some say power was only for the early church but I say let's learn and do more than the early church.

How, then, can we walk in the spirit and have this relationship with the Holy Spirit?

> *"But the comforter, which is the Holy Ghost, whom the Father will send in my name, he shall teach you all things; and bring all things to your remembrance, whatsoever I have said unto you."*
>
> **John 14: 26:26**

Who is this Spirit? Is he a person? Can I talk to him? How can I talk to him? Does he have a voice? Where does he live?

We are first introduced to the Spirit in Genesis 1:1 when we see him brooding over "the face of the deep" and we also see God saying commanding light and the Spirit acting upon God's word. The Spirit was part of creation. In Genesis 1:26, when God said "Let us make man in our own image," the "us" and "our" is inclusive of the Spirit, whom we can say is the powerhouse of God. He is the hand of God and the source of God's power.

The Holy Spirit has the same nature and attributes with God so you cannot separate the Holy Spirit from God just as you cannot separate Jesus from God.

In John 14:26, you begin to notice the nature of the Holy Spirit and how he can also indwell a believer. Jesus described the Holy Spirit as "another Comforter of the same kind". So the Holy Spirit can help you and comfort you just as Jesus did when he walked the earth.

The same way Jesus walked in Jerusalem is the same way the Holy Spirit is walking in our lives today. The same way Jesus talked with the people in his time is the same way the Holy Spirit is talking today. The challenge is how to relate with him because he lives in us and talks even through us if we allow him.

RELATING WITH THE SPIRIT

The Holy Spirit is already in the world and a part of the bride. All you need to do is ask him to come into your heart and talk to him when he is now a part of your life, like you would to your best friend or lover. His voice is made clearer when you understand God's word.
NB: The Holy Spirit speaks in line with the Father and the word. Get to know the Spirit and you will know the Father.

MAKE HIS SPIRIT LORD

The Spirit of God has come to testify of the word of God. You cannot know God outside of his word. When you understand the word you begin to understand the heart of God.

"But ye are come unto mount sion and unto mount sion, and unto the city of the living God, the heavenly Jerusalem and to an innumerable company of angels."

Hebrews 12:22

When many believers seek God, they look for a spectacular move of God rather than take his word as the highest level of understanding God. The book of Hebrews says that we have come into the company of innumerable angels. That scripture alone enables you to stand on God's word and say you have seen an angel because his word says you have come to Mt. Zion.

The Bible also contains a lot of angelic manifestations. When I look at how the angel Gabriel visited Mary, I celebrate because I have also seen him (angel Gabriel) in that scripture.

The word of God is more real than anything else in the world and if you allow God to show you the word and celebrate every encounter, you will begin to hear and understand the Spirit of God.

When the word becomes Lord, you are now fit for a life led by the Spirit, who usually points you to the word, the law manual or book of God's love – the letters of the Bible are what the bridegroom left the church so we can prepare for his second coming.

OTHER SPIRITS AND FALSE ANGELS

The reason why the Spirit leads you to God's word is so it can safely guide you from being led away from God. The Spirit of God leads man towards God's word and a relationship with God. The most amazing thing about the Holy Spirit is he perfects our relationship with God. Jesus came to restore us to God. The Holy Spirit and Jesus have come to help us approach God and to achieve a perfect relationship with God.

False angels can appear but Paul says in Galatians even if an angel is to tell you another gospel (other than what Paul had preached to them), let him be accursed.

In Genesis 6:2, the sons of God saw the daughters of men and came to meet with them and produced giants. This age is similar, just like in the days of Enoch, too, when fallen angels are communing with the church and producing false teachings and false spirits that are leading man astray. Enoch lived in this corrupt and evil time. He preached about the judgment of God because of the sinfulness of man. But the Enoch generation refuses to be corrupted by the false angel but choose to walk after the Spirit of God.

There is corruption, yes. There are already brothers who came in unawares in order to bring the church into bondage but the Enoch generation will walk by the word and correct all the strange doctrines and strange fires that are there, like those in the days of Enoch. This generation must execute judgment on the ungodly.

The Enoch generation draws people to the Bible. They will be a success but will not seek glory for themselves but point men to God. You can only separate the chaff from the wheat during harvest. So the only way you will be able to see who really are of God is by seeing the fruit. The Enoch generation manifests the fruit that come through fellowship with God.

The world is waiting for the manifestation of the sons of God and as these manifest the disciples will be drawn to Christ. The Enoch generation has to prove to the world what it means to walk with God. This generation should prove what it means to walk in the spirit.

The Spirit of God is ready to act through those who will not seek God for their glory but for his Glory.

CHAPTER 4

A CALL TO MEET THE LORD

T HE argument is not about when the Lord will come or how he will come, or even how we will go to heaven. The question is: has the Bride made herself ready to meet the Lord Jesus Christ?

Christians argue on doctrinal lines but the truth is Jesus is coming back soon and before his coming a call has gone out to all Christians and believers to demonstrate the benefits of fellowship with God. There is more to fellowship than what people think or assume. In this chapter, we are going to look at the idea of fellowship in great detail so that you may understand. It is my prayer that this knowledge will also help you develop your fellowship with God.

THE BENEFITS OF FELLOWSHIP

"Children in whom was no blemish, but well favored and skillful in all wisdom, and cunning in knowledge, and understanding, and such had ability in them to stand in the king's palace, and whom they might teach the learning of the Chaldean's."

Daniel 1:4

When you look at the life and ministry of Daniel, you realise that God will stand with you and grant you favour if you stand on his word. Daniel was the administrative assistant (in our days, the Prime Minister) of the land of Babylon, at that time the strongest nation in the known world. As I have indicated earlier, he served four different administrations. The most amazing thing about his story is that he was a perfect picture of the Enoch generation, full of wisdom and skill.

In Genesis chapters 5 to 10, we meet Noah, another perfect example of a man who walked with God. When you look at the ark of Noah, the level of ingenuity and craftiness transcends ordinary human skill.

In that generation, the world was corrupt. Noah walked with God as his great, great grandfather Enoch had done. I believe he could have learnt about his ancestor from his fathers. When you look at the life of Noah and the ark he built, you realise you can be innovative and ahead of your generation if you trust in God and tap into his vast reserve of knowledge and wisdom.

Jesus is coming for those who are a part of the world but not influenced by the world. These are people who are influencing the world for the Kingdom. We are called to be separated from the world, meaning those not influenced by the world or it systems.

If the company you work for does not subscribe to Christian ethos or promote the values of the faith, you are at risk of compromising just the way it happened in Sodom. If your country is led by non-believers, are they passing laws or regulations that support or promote Christian values? Am I saying leave that organisation? No, I am saying seek God and he will allow you to influence your world like Daniel who influenced kings to say there is no God like the God of Daniel who saves.

We should be in the leading roles in all positions of influence in the world so we can promote true Christian values. When television started the early church would call it Satan's box and failed to totally control the media of that time. As Christians, we are part of the world and we should study the trends in technological advancement. We should lead and be in full control of industries. It's time we take over. The world can only know there is JESUS and hell is real if we demonstrate Jesus in our world.

IS HELL REAL?

Yes. Those that will not be caught up to meet with the Lord in the air will be judged. They will be sent into the lake of fire. The desire of the Lord is that every man should be saved. He does not want anyone to go to hell and as we lead, we draw disciples to God and away from hell:

> "Let no man deceive you by any means: for that day shall not come, except there come the falling away first, and that man of sin be revealed, the son of perdition."
>
> **2 Thessalonians 2:3**

> "Let not any one deceive you in any manner, because [it will not be] unless the apostasy have first come, and the man of sin have been revealed, the son of perdition."
>
> **2 Thessalonians 2:3,**
> **Darby Translation**

The Bible speaks of a great falling away. When you look closely at the scripture, you begin to understand that before Christ comes, many shall fall away. Many will not believe in God or Jesus Christ. But the he Enoch generation shall walk in power and authority in a world that will be taken over by fallen angels and spirits that shall lead many astray. False prophets shall arise that will confuse many, leading them away from God. Other fallen angels will challenge the very existence of God as they will walk with power, making man believe in themselves and not God.

These spirits will demonstrate strange fires they will manifest power this world has not seen yet, which leads man to believe in his own ability. It shall be parallel to what the prophecy in Daniel, which speaks about the rock that will grow and influence the whole world, says.

There shall be gross darkness and the Enoch generation should be the light in this great time of falling away. The Enoch generation can only be a light if they walk in fellowship with God and this is through his word.

Warning: Many shall be drawn from the word as man shall preach from the vision they have seen and begin to add upon scripture. Let us as the Body of Christ stand on the word and not on our experiences of a vision we have seen. If we see visions, let them have scriptural foundation.

God does not want anyone to perish but man has ignored the voice of God and many shall perish on that day. The two parallels shall be the last events before the coming of Jesus. Like in the days of Enoch, there shall be a great falling away that caused God to send water that destroyed the world.

But during that time of sin and great falling away, Enoch walked with God. Enoch preached to the world by calling his son's name "judgment shall come".

Enoch walked with God just before the judgment and a generation is being called to walk with God just before the judgment that is coming. If this generation walks with God, it will be preserved like Noah was preserved in the flood.

Many shall go to hell yet the provision for salvation is for all man. It's a choice to follow God through Jesus or to live a life of sin. Can you be a man after God's heart and follow God in all your pursuits?

FOR THE LORD HIMSELF SHALL DESCEND FROM HEAVEN WITH A SHOUT, WITH THE VOICE OF THE ARCHANGEL AND WITH THE TRUMP OF GOD AND THE DEAD IN CHRIST SHALL RISE FIRST, THEN WE WHICH ARE ALIVE AND REMAIN SHALL BE CAUGHT UP TOGETHER WITH THEM IN THE CLOUDS TO MEET THE LORD IN

THE AIR AND SO SHALL WE EVER BE WITH THE LORD.

1 THESSALONIANS 4:16-17

Surely the Lord will come and those that believed in him will be caught up to meet him in the air. This is the rapture of the church – Christians who would have believed in Christ and had fellowship with God. This fellowship is a relationship with our Creator through Jesus Christ. The bride (the church) of Christ has not agreed on when shall the rapture occur and how it shall happen. They are divided on doctrinal lines. But I want you to understand the rapture will happen and it will happen to the Enoch generation, a generation of believers who walk with God.

ARE YOU READY?

---

25 Then shall the kingdom of heaven be likened unto ten virgins, which took their lamps, and went forth to meet the bridegroom.
² And five of them were wise, and five were foolish.

³ They that were foolish took their lamps, and took no oil with them:

⁴ But the wise took oil in their vessels with their lamps.

⁵ While the bridegroom tarried, they all slumbered and slept.

⁶ And at midnight there was a cry made, Behold, the bridegroom cometh; go ye out to meet him.

⁷ Then all those virgins arose, and trimmed their lamps.

⁸ And the foolish said unto the wise, Give us of your oil; for our lamps are gone out.

⁹ But the wise answered, saying, Not so; lest there be not enough for us and you: but go ye rather to them that sell, and buy for yourselves.

¹⁰ And while they went to buy, the bridegroom came; and they that were ready went in with him to the marriage: and the door was shut.

¹¹ Afterward came also the other virgins, saying, Lord, Lord, open to us.

¹² But he answered and said, Verily I say unto you, I know you not.

¹³ Watch therefore, for ye know neither the day nor the hour wherein the Son of man cometh.

Jesus, in this parable, shows us the two groups of people in the world today – those prepared and full of the Spirit and those who are not aglow with the Spirit of God. Which group do you belong to? Are you ready for the soon-coming king? Have you made yourself ready for the bridegroom? The five that had oil made it to the wedding feast. Do you have oil? Do you have a relationship with the Holy Spirit who, in our time, is this oil? Do you know him? Have you now understood how he speaks?

Here is the final call. Have you accepted the call to fellowship and have you prepared for his second coming? Jesus is coming back soon and you have a job to demonstrate to your world what it means to fellowship with God and what it does to you...

CLOSING PRAYER

Lord, help me to walk perfectly before you and allow me to have a relationship with you until your

return .keep me from falling and help me demon-strate you in my home work place and church...
AMEN

www.ingramcontent.com/pod-product-compliance
Lightning Source LLC
LaVergne TN
LVHW010031070426
835508LV00005B/293